For My Sons

A Poem By Jeannette Ayala Eseberre

*T*o my sons,
Larry and Anthony.
Although you're too big for me to cradle in my lap now,
you'll always be my babies.

*T*o my husband, Larry
Thank you for all of your hard work,
and for giving our family a beautiful life.

My children are my treasures,
God's greatest gift to me

I want for them the beauties of life,
and a loving world to see

I cannot always protect them,
or keep them away from pain

B*ut I can guide them in the right direction,*
so wisdom they will gain

I feed them, clothe them, bathe them, and provide them a safe home

I hug them, kiss them, and love them,
so caring they will know

*M*y loving hopes and wishes are prayed for them each day

*T*hese are the things I say to them
to help them find their way

*W*hen you have friends in your life,
be sure to treat each other right

Don't judge, don't gossip, and don't lie or do things out of spite

Those you feel are true at heart
are the friends you want to keep

The ones who try to tear you down
are those you need to leave

*R*emember what God says,
"Do unto others as you would have done to you."

*B*elieve me, my sons, your good deeds will be reflected back to you

Be smart and be kind, but try to
understand the ways of the world today

Be honest, be true, do what YOU want to do, just do it in an honorable way

*W*hen you choose a love in your life,
be sure they love you for you

*I*t will be especially important in marriage
when you become one instead of two

No matter what our ups and downs might be, the fact will always remain

The love I have for you, my beautiful sons, will forever be the same

So for now, kiss me goodnight,
and may you have sweet dreams

Please thank God for our blessings, and
I'll thank Him for bringing you both to me